Foreword by Neil Samu

When facing death it's natural to look back at your life and reflect on the choices you have made and the people you have loved or lost, the times of great joy or profound sadness and your hopes and desires for those closest to you after you depart this mortal coil.

Robert Murphy is a man that has lived his life with love and laughter, he has a joyous spirit, a wicked sense of humour, a wonderful caring family and truly loyal if somewhat crazy friends.

This book has been written using eye gaze technology as an aggressive form of MND has insidiously consumed his body but not his mind

His diagnosis was 18th months but over 3 years later he is still with us and has seen his daughter get married, overcome covid, twice, and been delighted to welcome his grandson into the world.

"The true measure of a man is not how he behaves in moments of comfort and convenience but how he stands at times of controversy and challenges." — **Martin Luther King Jr**

Introduction

I first noticed something wasn't right about March April 2017. Playing football I could feel I wasn't running right and I noticed I couldn't open water bottle tops the strength had gone from my fingers. Then during the summer I noticed the fasciculations in my arms where my muscles were twitching. I went to the gp and she was quite upset when we spoke as I had already googled my symptoms and knew that it could be MND.

I was sent to Frimley in November to see a neurological specialist who although she did say she was 90% sure I would need to see one of the professors of MND in Oxford.

I saw him in January 2018 and after a check he said yes you definitely have it and it seems aggressive. I was told that most people survive about 3 years and I could expect about 18 months I had to leave my flat in March 2019 and moved into the care home then. Also that week I had an operation to have the peg fitted which is the feeding tube in my stomach.

My daughter got married in July 2021 after having it cancelled twice due to covid. Their son Benno was born 3rd June 2022. Both of these I never thought I would see.

I got covid twice but the first time was in January 2020 a very hard time and we unfortunately lost three residents but somehow I made it through, but it was close.

Well I'm still here and I should mention that I am so grateful for all the help I've had but without the eye gaze technology I would never have attempted these poems. I hope you enjoy reading them.

This book is dedicated to my brother Stephen 'Spud' Murphy, who will always be loved and remembered.

Best wishes Rob

Yesterday's Man

I hear the angels wings beating round my
door
But the devil's are crawling across the floor
If I walk with Jesus he will save my soul
I can pray all day but I just don't know

I could doesn't mean I would
And if I don't doesn't mean I won't
The chances that went by
Doesn't mean I didn't try
You try your best
Fate takes care of the rest
The world will turn without you and I.

Feelings and dreams important to me
People from past memories
The warmth of an altered reality
The beautiful autumnal leaves
Twisting and dancing down to the ground
On a cold invisible breeze
The seasons and dreams of yesterday's
man
Dismissed and no one believes.

Beautiful Friend

Bright and breezy September day,
 Autumn changes underway.
The sunlight dappled reflections through the windows.
I swam in my darkness lonely in the crowd,
Laughing and joking, my desperate shroud.
And then you were there my beautiful friend.

We spoke, we laughed, you told me your name,
I knew at that moment things wouldn't be the same.
The sun had now dipped the evening crept in.
My shroud slipped away, my heart on amend,
The day I met my beautiful friend.

Her smile, her eyes, her inner spark,
Her movements, her curves, lighting up my dark.
We shared hopes and fears and spoke of dreams.
All invitations were politely declined
By a friend whose beauty was also refined.

Time passes quickly it's never enough,
The end comes nearer and I can't call it's bluff.
Now the sun's lost its warmth the cold is creeping in,
But I'll always love my beautiful friend.

The Take

The wait, the take, She made me feel fake.

The hold, the touch, I loved her so much.

The hopes, the fears, She left me with tears.

The memories of time I try to flee,
but I know in my heart she really loved me.

Weights and Measures

I don't want to dive to the depths of my
mind,

I don't want to know the things I might find.
Should I relate my biggest fears
Or leave them buried amongst the years.
I feel I've been hung, drawn and quartered,
Neutered, abandoned and slaughtered.
What is left for me everything comes to an
end,
There is nowhere left to turn, no rules left to
bend.

The drag of the tick, the weight of the tock,
The monotonous chime of an imperious
clock.
Measuring thoughts that shouldn't be
measured,
Loves and dreams that must be treasured.

I won't be leaving with the things that I'd
hoped for,
But somehow I think I have found so much
more.

Mother Earth

The wave rising high dives for the beach,
Pushing and stretching but just out of reach.
Rolling away, another crashes in,
An endless pursuit with a will to win.

The sun is smiling like some Jekyll and Hyde,
He'll keep his hat on as the earth is fried.
Waters rising and islands drown,
Mother knows who wears the crown.

Like the trees reaching for the sky,
We live and grow seldom asking why.
Do we think we have the final say,
Chaos and nature will have the day.

We have to let the oil flow,
Petrodollars are the way to go.
And all the time we know,
We reap what we sow.

Future Memories

What colour will your eyes be?

What wonders will you see?
How will your hair grow, straight or curly?
Will you arrive late or will you be early?

What would you want Father Christmas to
bring you?
Will you look at the stars and be enchanted
too?
Will you love music, sports and stuff?
Will you be strong when things get tough?

Will you travel and see what the world has to
give?
Will you be happy where you are and love
where you live?
Will you get married and live happily ever
after?
Will you run down a beach screaming with
laughter?

I just want you to love and laugh and always
try your best,
I want you to be yourself and always feel
blessed.

And when your mum hugs you tight I
hope you can see
That like your mum you'll always carry
a little piece of me.

The Key

When faced with your own mortality,

You play a part in the worst self tragedy,
Something like a black comedy,
Written by a master of parody.

Chasing me through my dreams, a spectral
dude,
Sprinting in slow motion, my words all
skewed.
I'm screwed and conclude, forever pursued.
I awake with a feeling of gratitude.

Hope is the key, the thing that drives me,
It sets me free to believe that we could kiss
under the shade of an old oak tree.
I see what we could be, creating my own
personal destiny.
It's been a while since I saw your smile,
I'd swim a sea mile or do any trial,
It would be worthwhile to spend time with
you, lily of the Nile.

I won't close the door on what went before,
I want more of this L'Amour,
It's not a cure but helps me endure.

The Beauty of the Deep

The weight of the afternoon on
my eyes

The smothering feeling of sleep
The deliverance from these lies
The beauty of the deep

Sunlight burns through my
mind
Keeping me in touch
With a world I want to leave
behind
The dreams I need so much

I still feel reality around me
My conscience far away
Spirit dancing easy and free
I wish I could make it stay

But those afternoon dreams soon
depart
With a promise to come back and
sooth my heart.

Celebrating the wedding of Simon and Emma,

Building a home and a family together.
You see a mother of two lovely girls,
I remember the girl with her hair full of curls.

As you grew up with your dancing and singing,
Never aware of the joy you were bringing.
Running, skipping and plenty of twirls,
Big blue eyes with your hair full of curls.

Simon, Ava and Isla your gorgeous family,
The future is bright that is plain to see.
Now we wait as the next chapter unfurls
For the lovely bride with the beautiful curls.

I'm not the only one who wishes I could be there,
To celebrate the wedding of the girl with curls in her hair

Undone

The dances we danced and the songs we had sung,

The smiles and glances and all of the fun,

Places we travelled some so far flung,

Morning dew and the rising sun,

The love that we shared when I was the one,

Every day just like we had begun,

I didn't see what you saw, what we had become,

Words thrown around and nobody won,

The mess that was left as it all came undone.

Special Wedding

Love conquers all, so the proverb says,

It's crowning glory these wedding days.
Everyone dressing up in their finest clothes,
And all in white, the bride, a vision, a rose.

Aphrodite, the goddess of love,
Put these two together, a blessing from above.
A gorgeous young couple become man and wife,
Moving forward to an exciting new life.

–

I've watched you grow from a tiny babe in arms,
Now a woman, beautiful, intelligent an abundance of
charms.
Let's celebrate this day now, it's a wonderful thing,
To dance, to eat, to drink and sing.

I look at you now with enormous pride and I really
want it said,
I love you more than anything,
The day my daughter got wed.

Another Country

A different country with sunshine hues,

Ripened yellow and deep azure blues.
Shangri - la hotel, room for the past,
Bad memories discarded fast.

A martyr, his glorious loneliness,
The misery of her happiness.
A haunting victory that lasts for years
Preceded by a flood of tears.
Old photographs and black and white stills
Always wanting love, even though love kills.

Degradation, desperation the hell of this situation,
Everyday I make a choice, today I'll put my smiley
face on.
I'm here someplace not there
Never leaving my head, not saying where.

I'll retire now to my shangri-la
Inside my mind and yet so far.

Raindrops

The silver tops of translucent raindrops

Run down my window in a race that never stops.
Reflecting on years that passed so fast
How and why the die was cast.

Did we turn corners or walk endless straight roads,
Joyous possibilities of youthful episodes.
The sun is now setting on last year's parade,
Reds lose their vigour, pinks start to fade.

Love's arrival heralds a powerful rush,
Exciting, inspiring then inhibiting us.
I've heard that word a thousand times but never from
your lips,
Hearts very slowly torn apart in ever increasing strips.

Happiness comes from within, don't look to others for
it,
Just live and love and laugh and smile and never ever
quit.

No One Knows

Don't look at me for the answers,

You will find your own peace inside.
Ignore the liars, cheats and chancers,
They're looking to take you for a ride.
Tales of kingdoms and great pits of fire,
Astral pathways and pulsating bright lights,
Warm dreams taking you higher,
Vortex of thoughts and beautiful sights.

I will rest beneath a great English oak
And join the world around me.
I will be in the grass the rain will soak,
I will be in the air the land the sea.

My soul, my conscience won't be found,
Thoughts, feelings and dreams all disappear.
What happens to them, the question goes around
No one knows, the answers unclear.

Is Love a Cliché

Does love really break your heart

Do you always know what this means
My thoughts tear my mind apart
You appear to me in all my dreams

How can the sea touch the sky
Do you feel melancholy in the rain
I search for the truth with a watery eye
And untie the knot in the wallowing pain

Cards, notes and love heart props
A stream of conscious that keeps on flowing
Where are you left when the penny drops
Travelling one way but don't know where you're going

The life and loves of a cliched man
Sleep peacefully now you did all you can

What is Within

Memories, thoughts or feelings. Whatever they are,

Swimming around inside me, never too far.
These feelings reside within me,
Sparked into life by something I see.

A ray of light breaking through my window,
Taking me places I used to go.
Or something I hear or smell,
Stirs up the house where memories dwell.

A song or a note, that a stranger wrote,
Will make these feelings bubble up and float
to the surface with a golden glow,
In my mind or in my heart, I never know.

Sometimes in my stomach with an ancient longing,
Through my body with a sense of belonging.
The autumn leaves baring winter trees,
Bring Christmas past, midnight mass and a boy who
believes.

Reminiscing

I'd see you around and that was the start,
Romeo and Juliet, we both played our part.
A bunch of kids together we had a great little gang,
But you and me together, a heavenly yin and yang.

We soon grew close, as close as we could be,
We had no worries, no responsibility.
Dirk Wears White Sox and Hunky Dory,
A wonderful time, a teenage story.

There was nothing to regret, there was no reason why,
No last phone call, no lingering goodbye.
We just seemed to grow apart, teenagers sometimes do,
No more hanging together and the years they just flew.

The smile in your eyes as you walked through my door,
Took me rushing back forty years or more.
A relished memory from my far distant past,
Like a well-loved actress re-joining the cast.

We sat down in the garden and we got on so well,
The time that had passed you never could tell.
Smiles and laughter returning so fast,
The feelings we had made, they were made to last.

PRECIOUS TIME

I feel I'm wasting precious time but what else can I
do,
I feel days are rushing past me and I only have a few.
I dream of people and places that once upon a time I
knew,
And now and again when the stars align sometimes I
dream of you.

I can't say that you are right and maybe I am wrong,
I think I am writing a novel but it's probably just a
song.
I see the same things you do as we stand side by side,
I want to run towards it and you want to run and hide.

I open doors and windows someplace in my mind,
The things I think I'm looking for I never seem to find.
No one would choose to be alone and no one wants to
die,
But what is the truth for someone else, just leaves me
asking why.

Life is full of contradictions and love has more than its
share,
I move along the best I can, I don't judge what is right
or fair.

Two 7s Clash

 Two skinny young kids strolling down the Strand,

Going down to see the greatest rock n roll band.
Lady London we were free to roam,
Safe inside our European home.
We'd jump on trains and buses and run down the tracks,
Always making sure we had each other's backs.
If anyone told us that we were shot
We'd laugh and sing "don't push us when we're hot".

We stuck together through thick and thin,
Different people but the same within.
You had talent in abundance,
Butch Cassidy to my Sundance.
We took different paths to try our luck,
But if music could talk, the words had stuck.

Now no one gets this far without any joy or pain
To appreciate the sun you have to taste the rain.
When the waves crashed over the bow far out in the Med,
In the Indian ocean where the skies turned red.
Big Sur, Venice Beach and San Francisco,
There was nowhere we couldn't go.

When I'm gone and you travel to places,
Remember the fun and our smiling faces.
We should be jumping shouting that we made it all this way,
From Hayes Town station to drinking in L. A.

When time runs out and we get to the end,
Thank you my brother, my confidant , my friend.
And when you look at the sky and remember me,
Go it easy, step lightly, stay free.

Everything I Am

You have always been like a gift from above,

Filling my life with comfort and love.
All the things that a child would need,
The sun and water growing a seed.

How did I get so lucky to have a mum like you,
Full of love, warmth and funny to.
Always at my side, when I've wanted to hide.
It's your strength you see in me now,
I learnt it from you when I didn't know how.

Looking adversity straight in the face,
Keep your head high and act with grace.
Don't fall apart when life makes you sad,
You will get through it, it won't be so bad.
Don't fight battles that can never be won,
Time and patience will put you back in the sun.

Everything good you see in me,
Is down to you and who you made me be.
I have always felt like I'm the lucky one,
Because you are my mother and I love being your
son.

Free

It's a lot slower than I thought but faster than I'd like,
  Like running in a dream or going uphill on a bike.
  I can still hear the music although the party has
finished, I will keep on shining although my light has
diminished.

  I will never walk again on a warm faraway beach,
  The things I want to do are now so far out of reach.
  I'd like to hold you tight and whisper in your ear,
  But that will never happen now, those words you'll
never hear.

  Maybe now I'm free from these thoughts that never
really last,
  Free from my future, free from my present and free
from my past.
  I often wonder where I'm going with this,
  Should I say some more or just give it a miss.

  I'm addicted to read the shite that you write about
how life was so good in the past,
  And I want to tell you that just isn't true but I really
just can't be arsed.

CHP227209-1
This book was created at solentro.co.uk
The responsible publisher is Rob Murphy.